ORIGAMI *for*
Harmony and Happiness

幸福と調和を
招く折り紙

ORIGAMI *for*
Harmony and Happiness

幸福と調和を
招く折り紙

STEVE and MEGUMI BIDDLE

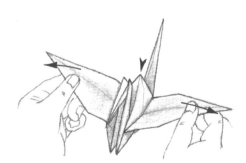

CONNECTIONS
BOOK PUBLISHING

A CONNECTIONS EDITION
This edition published in Great Britain in 2003 by
Connections Book Publishing Limited
St Chad's House, 148 King's Cross Road, London WC1X 9DH

British Library Cataloguing-in-Publication data available on request.

ISBN 1-85906-114-1

10 9 8 7 6 5 4 3 2

Phototypeset in Amazone BT, Stone and Folio using QuarkXPress
on Apple Macintosh
Origination by Pixel Tech, Singapore
Printed by Hung Hing Offset Printing Co. Ltd, China

Contents

縁起物

干支を折る

四神の霊力

Foreword

*Welcome to the fabulous world of origami, the art of paper folding. Origami can be enjoyed by anybody, regardless of age, nationality or language. Each year more and more people are joining the growing numbers of enthusiasts exploring the pleasures of origami. Now, this art takes on a new dimension; one that brings paper folding back to its oriental origins. In **Origami for Harmony and Happiness**, paper folding meets feng shui and Chinese astrology.*

There is more to origami than just folding paper; there is magic in transforming a flat square of paper into a three-dimensional piece of art, breathing life into an otherwise static object. The very act of folding stimulates and enriches the imagination, creating ideas and improving hand and eye coordination. Such focus calls for a Zen-like concentration, a meditation that can also create an enormous sense of calm and relaxation. For when our attention is fully engaged, the mind becomes silent; when we succeed in restricting our thoughts to one subject, the incessant internal chattering stops. Indeed, the contentment we feel when our minds are absorbed often comes less from the activity itself, than from the fact that in concentrating, our worries or problems are forgotten.

   Like many traditional books on origami, this one includes models of animals, birds, flowers and decorative objects. What sets this book apart is the inspiration the objects create. The projects are based on concepts selected from the world of feng shui and Chinese astrology, each of which has a particular significance. And when the meditative

幸福と調和を招く折り紙

skills of paper folding are combined with the practice, philosophy and principles of feng shui, we can create tranquillity in the home or office and promote harmony in the mind and body and in the environment around us.

Origami promotes the joy of giving and receiving. A paper sculpture is created and given to a friend as a gift (the way it is presented can say a lot about the care and thought that went into its creation). The friend learns the skill and makes another model, and so the craft, the desire to learn and share, and the gesture of friendship are all perpetuated.

Finally, we would like to echo the words of our very good origami friends, the late Lillian Oppenheimer of New York City and Toshie Takahama of Tokyo, Japan: always remember that the real secret of origami lies in the giving and the sharing with others. We hope you'll discover a harmonious relationship between the many creative possibilities of origami and the exciting principles of feng shui.

Steve and Megumi Biddle

午　未　申　酉　戌　亥

The Origins of Origami

The ancient Chinese were the inventors of paper, its origin being attributed to Tsai Lun, in the year 105 CE. The main tradition of paper folding in China was discovered within the Chinese tradition of funerary art, in which replicas or representations of money or household goods are tossed onto coffins as symbols of objects for the departed to take with them into the next world.

For more than five hundred years, the Chinese kept the art of making paper a secret. Then in the eighth century, Chinese invaders who were captured in Arabia were forced to reveal the technique. Eventually the process reached southern Europe. The Spanish symbol of paper folding – the *pajarita*, or 'little bird' – is said to have existed in the seventeenth century. Elsewhere in Europe, paper folding took place in the form of decorative napkin folds.

Paper-making methods where introduced into Japan (from China, by way of Korea) with the spread of Buddhism during the Asuka era (593–686). The missionaries used paper for the inscription of *sutras* – Buddhist prayers – and so spread, not only 'the word', but also the medium upon which it was written. It is also interesting to note that the Japanese word *kami* can mean 'God', as well as 'paper'. The two meanings are distinguished by the characters, which are written differently. This has given rise to a belief that paper is sacred. It has long been associated with the Shinto religion and the folding of *hitogata* – human figures – that are blessed by God.

Origami in everyday life

Origami wasn't practised for personal enjoyment during ancient times, because paper was scarce and therefore very valuable. It probably became a little more widespread during the Heian period (794–1185), with the development of elaborate ceremonial and recreational paper folds. During the Muromachi period (1333–1568), origami styles served to distinguish the aristocratic samurai from the lower-class farmers and peasants. As this period was one of military rule, people knew their place in society, and therefore they folded accordingly. It was during the Edo period (1600–1868), a time of development in

the arts, that paper became inexpensive enough for everyone to use it, and origami then became a form of entertainment. Woodblock prints from this period show origami models, people folding paper, and origami shapes in kimono patterns.

In the 1890s, the Japanese government introduced a widespread system of preschool education, and origami was introduced as a tool for bringing minds and hands into coordination. It is still taught to young children today. Origami is now gaining respect as a valuable creative activity, receiving patronage from both Japanese industry and cultural institutions.

Origami and the Western world

The development of paper folding in the West can be traced back to a troupe of Japanese jugglers who visited Europe in the 1860s, soon after Japan's long period of isolation had ended with the Meiji restoration. The jugglers brought with them the method for folding the 'flapping bird'. Soon, directions for this and other folds were appearing in various European publications. Magicians including Harry Houdini and Robert Harbin were especially interested in paper folding, attesting to the link between origami and magic, which continues today.

Since the 1950s, interest in origami has proliferated in the United States and Great Britain as well as Japan, resulting in a variety of books and articles on the subject and in the founding of many origami societies worldwide (*see Useful Addresses, page 96*). Today, new and improved folding procedures have led to the creation of models that would have astounded the old origami masters. Where once it was considered almost impossible to fold a lifelike insect that gave the impression of a body, antennae and legs, anatomically correct ones are now considered commonplace. Happily, however, not all paper folders have reduced origami to achievements of technical skill. The artistry and purity of folding paper still flourishes.

What is Feng Shui?

*The characters that translate into the words **feng shui** mean 'wind and water'. Feng shui is the ancient Chinese science of arranging everything around us in a way that will enable us to live in greater harmony with our environment. It can mean different things to different people. Feng shui does not contradict any religious or cultural understanding; it is the discipline of bringing together mankind and the environment in which we live. It also teaches us that with guidance we can control our fate in a positive way, thus alleviating misfortune.*

Chi energy

Feng shui teaches the art of channelling *chi*, or 'life force' into our lives, thereby obtaining peace and harmony. Chi embraces everything and holds together all aspects of feng shui. The chi energy you take in from your environment influences your moods, emotions, physical energy and, over time, your health. It is a force that flows all around and within and is sometimes called 'dragon's cosmic breath'.

Feng shui has been practised in China since at least the Tang Dynasty (618–907). It was originally practised by the Chinese Masters for the Emperors and their families, the elite and the rich. The ordinary person engaged in it on pain of death. From such beginnings, feng shui gradually became available to the masses as those who had the knowledge felt that it should not be kept solely for the privileged few. Master Yang Yum Sang, who is universally acknowledged as the founder of feng shui, left behind a legacy of classical texts that have been preserved and which continue to be studied to this day. In China, feng shui was, and is, practised a great deal, save only for a comparatively brief and enforced break during the Cultural Revolution.

Today, in many areas of Asia, feng shui is part of everyday life with both businesses and individuals regularly calling upon the services of a feng shui consultant. With Asians now living all over the world, their traditions are becoming more and more widespread, and it is now possible to find feng shui consultants in most major towns and cities.

Feng Shui and Colour

Feng shui uses colour as a symbol, the strongest colours being red, green and gold, which are used in many Chinese decorations.

Red warmth, prosperity, stimulation, happiness, festivity
Green peace, eternity, harmony
Gold royalty, strength, wealth
Silver wealth, success, beauty
Yellow enlightenment, intellect, gaiety
Blue heaven, peacefulness, stability (dark blue is linked with water)
Pink happiness, romance
White purity, peace, mourning (sometimes)
Brown safety, stability, elegance
Purple passion, motivation, spirituality
Black strength, misfortune, charm
Orange intellect, happiness, concentration

Feng shui uses the five elements of wood, fire, earth, metal and water. Paper is associated with wood. The elements are used extensively, to create and adjust energy and also to show how energy can affect chi in ourselves, the home and the universe around us.

Helpful Tips

Before you begin any of the projects in this book, read through the following tips designed to make origami easier.

- Before you start, make sure your paper is the correct shape.

- Do your folding on a smooth, flat surface such as a table or a book. Ensure that your folds are neat and accurate.

- Press your folds into place with your thumbnail.

- In the diagrams in this book, the shading represents the coloured side of the paper.

- Look at each diagram carefully, read the instructions, then look at the next diagram to see what shape should be created when you have completed the step you are working on.

- You will find it easiest to work your way through from the beginning of the book to the end, as some of the projects and procedures in later sections are based partially on previous ones. However, if you are an experienced paper folder and can follow origami instructions without too much help, feel free to select any design as a starting point.

- Most of the models can be folded from one square of paper, but a few require more. The instructions at the start of each project clearly state what you will need. If you are using your own paper rather than the paper supplied with this book, make sure it is cut absolutely square. There is nothing more frustrating than trying to fold a nearly square square!

- Above all, if a fold or whole model does not work out, don't give up hope. Go through the illustrations one by one, checking that you have read the instructions correctly. If you are still unable to complete the model, put it to one side and come back to it later with a fresh mind.

Symbols and the Basics of Folding

The symbols that form the basis of the instructions in this book are used internationally. They show the direction in which the paper should be folded. If you are new to origami, we suggest that you take a few squares of paper and study the following symbols and folding procedures before trying any of the origami projects. Look at the diagrams carefully to see which way the dashes, dots and arrows go over, through and under the paper, and fold your paper accordingly.

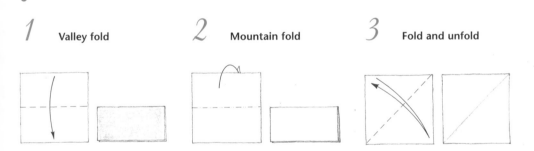

1 Valley fold

A valley fold (fold towards you or in front) is shown by a line of dashes and a solid arrow showing the direction in which the paper has to be folded.

2 Mountain fold

A mountain fold (fold away from you or behind) is shown by a line of dots and dashes and a hollow-headed arrow. As in the valley fold, the arrow shows the direction in which the paper has to be folded.

3 Fold and unfold

An arrow that comes back on itself means fold, press flat and unfold the paper back to its previous position.

4 Step fold

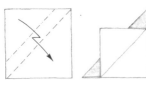

A zigzagged arrow drawn on top of the diagram means fold the paper in the direction shown by the arrow. A step fold is made by pleating the paper in a valley and mountain fold.

5 Fold over and over

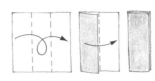

A looped arrow drawn on top of a diagram means keep folding the paper over in the direction shown by the arrow. Each fold-line represents one fold-over move.

6 Outside reverse fold

Solid and hollow-headed arrows, and valley and mountain fold-lines instruct you to separate the layers of paper, taking one to the front and one to the back.

10 Turn around

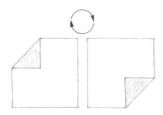

Two circling arrows means turn the paper (or model) around into the position shown.

11 Cut

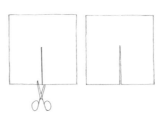

A pair of scissors and a solid line means cut the paper. The solid line shows the position of the cut.

12 Insert

An arrow with the tail broken near the head means insert the point into the pocket as shown.

7 Inside reverse fold

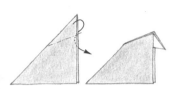

A wavy arrow with a broken tail and a mountain fold-line means pull the point inside the model, in the direction indicated by the wavy arrow.

8 Open and squash

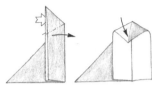

A hollow arrow with a short, indented tail instructs you to open out the layers of paper and squash them down neatly into the position shown in the following diagram.

9 Turn over

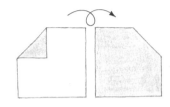

A looped arrow means turn the paper (or model) over in the direction shown.

13 Blow

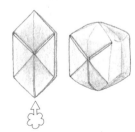

A hollow arrow with a cloud-like tail instructs you to blow where the arrow indicates. This symbol is used when a particular fold has to be inflated ...

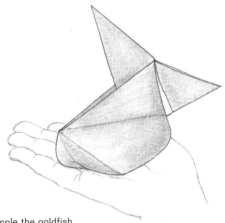

... for example the goldfish

GOOD LUCK SYMBOLS

Auspicious feng shui is connected to certain symbols and objects because of their colouring, the materials from which they have been created, or because their Chinese names are relevant to issues such as long life, peace or good fortune. Excellent areas to display such items are the living room, dining room, bedroom, study and the front entrance to the home.

Objects of art that are rich in feng shui qualities, or are associated with feng shui, can help to repel negative energy when displayed in the home or workplace. Good luck symbols placed or hung along dark and narrow corridors will encourage a flow of prosperous chi to meander through them.

The following origami models are favourite subjects for Asian artists to depict, and they are found on fabrics, screens, fans, vases and sculptures, as well as paintings and prints. Have fun folding them, while at the same time discovering their feng shui symbolism and reaping the good fortune they will bring into your life.

縁起物

蛙と蓮の葉

蓮華

鶴

金魚

鴛鴦

ハート

Heart

Feng shui can bring positive energy to romance and marriage, smoothing over and enhancing relationships and so bringing happiness into your life. Red heart shapes, as excellent symbols of romance, can be used to encourage good marriage prospects.

According to the principles of feng shui, every home has a marriage corner. This is represented by the southwestern part of the house. Any issues relating to marriage should be dealt with here. Decorate the area with symbols of wedded bliss, such as mandarin ducks, hearts and red roses. Display the items in pairs to represent a couple.

ハート

赤いハートは恋愛の印
一対のハートは夫婦愛を呼ぶ

17

Making Your Heart

As this model is flat, it can be contained in an envelope together with your love letters or greetings cards. It would also make an ideal place card for a romantic dinner. Use a square piece of paper, white side up.

1

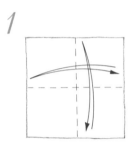

Crease the middle fold-lines as shown.

2

Valley fold the bottom corners up and the top edge down, so they meet the middle fold-lines.

3

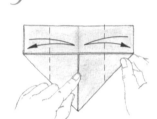

Fold and unfold the sides as shown.

7

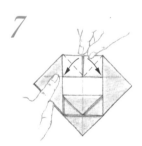

Valley fold the middle corners to meet their adjacent vertical edges.

8

Valley fold each top point down a little. Fold and unfold the side points as shown.

9

Inside reverse fold the side points along the fold-lines made in step 8.

4

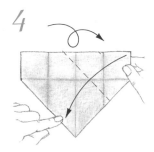

Turn the paper over. Valley fold the top right-hand corner, so it meets the opposite sloping edge as shown.

5

Valley fold the top left-hand corner, so it meets the opposite sloping edge.

6

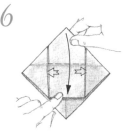

Open out the two side pockets slightly, and valley fold the top point down along the horizontal fold-line. Press the paper flat.

10

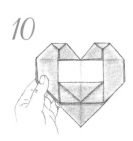

This should be the result.

11

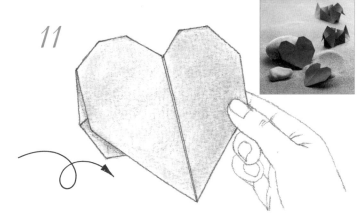

Turn the paper over to admire your finished heart.

Goldfish

In traditional Chinese culture, water, and the creatures that live in it, are believed to bring prosperity. In the home, an odd number of goldfish kept together is particularly auspicious. This will often include one black fish to draw away negative energy and provide protection. The combination of eight goldfish plus one black one, for example, is used in feng shui to encourage the healthy flow of chi around the home and for promoting wealth.

In the commercial world, an aquarium of small darting fish generates energy and new ideas, while larger, slower species can be used to create a calm atmosphere in locations such as doctors' waiting rooms.

金魚

奇数の金魚は手運を呼び、一匹の黒出目金は運を操く

Making Your Goldfish

This captivating origami model is thought to have originated in China. Use a square piece of paper, white side up.

1

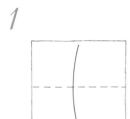

Valley fold the square in half from top to bottom.

2

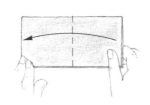

Valley fold the paper in half from right to left.

3

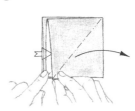

Lift the top half up, open out the paper and …

4

… squash it down neatly …

5

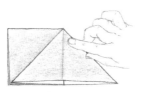

… into a triangle.

6

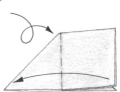

Turn the paper over. Repeat steps 2 to 5, to make a waterbomb base.

7

Take the top layer and valley fold the bottom points up to meet the top point.

8

Valley fold the side points in to the middle.

9

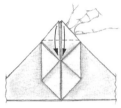

Valley fold the top points in to the middle, to make two triangular flaps at the top.

13

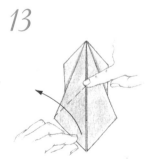

Valley fold the bottom left-hand fin over and outward into the position shown in step 14.

14

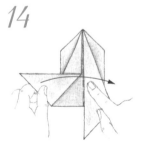

Valley fold the left-hand fin over to the right, as though turning the page of a book.

15

Hold the paper between fingers and thumbs with the small hole that is located at the base of the fins facing you. Place your lips right up to the paper and blow gently into the hole, which ...

10

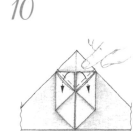

Tuck these flaps into the adjacent pockets with a valley fold.

11

Your model should now look like this.

12

Turn the paper over. From the top point, valley fold the sloping edges in to meet the middle fold-line, making the tail fins.

16

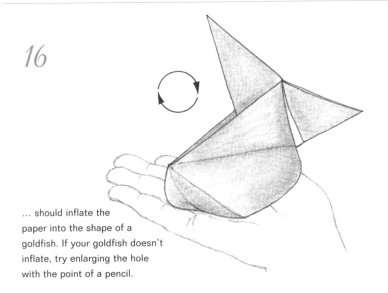

... should inflate the paper into the shape of a goldfish. If your goldfish doesn't inflate, try enlarging the hole with the point of a pencil.

Mandarin Duck

In feng shui, the mandarin duck is a symbol of marital happiness, as it mates for life. A pair of ducks is particularly powerful. Like the heart, its most prominent position is in the southwestern part of the home.

The mandarin duck can also be used in other areas of feng shui. Placed in the north of your home it will have a real influence in business mergers. If positioned in the west, it will bring good luck to the marriages of the householder's children.

鴛鴦

一対の鴛鴦は夫婦間の幸福を象徴する

24

Making Your Mandarin Duck

The following model should help you to understand inside and outside reverse folds. Use a square piece of paper, coloured side up.

1

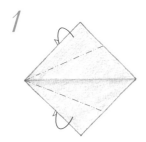

Crease the middle fold-line as shown. From the left-hand point, mountain fold the sloping edges behind to meet the middle fold-line, making a kite base.

2

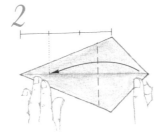

Valley fold the right-hand point over to the left as far as shown.

3

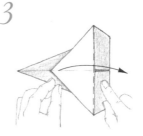

Valley fold the point back out to the right.

4

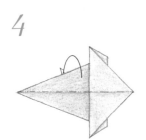

Mountain fold the paper in half from top to bottom.

5

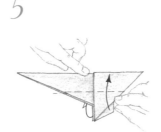

Valley fold the bottom point up, to make a wing. Repeat behind.

6

Fold and unfold the left-hand point into the position shown by the dotted lines.

7

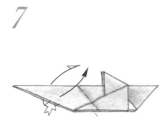

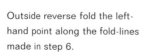

Outside reverse fold the left-hand point along the fold-lines made in step 6.

8

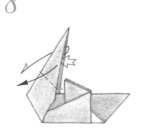

Again, outside reverse fold the point, so it points to the left, making the duck's head and beak.

9

Step fold the beak on either side as shown. Inside reverse fold the right-hand point down.

10

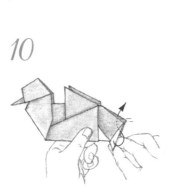

Inside reverse fold the point back up, to make the duck's tail.

11

Your mandarin duck is complete.

Lily Pad and Frog

According to the principles of feng shui, green leaves create their own distinctive flow of chi energy. Pointed leaves help the flow of chi move quickly, while floppy, rounded leaves create a calming flow of chi. Filling the house with freshly cut blooms encourages lucky chi, while dying and dead flowers will lure illness and bad luck. Computers and other electrical goods have a negative effect on the flow of healthy chi. Thriving, colourful flowers or plants placed nearby will help prevent this.

蛙と蓮の葉

Frogs are used in feng shui to inspire quick thinking, fast reactions and great leaps of activity. They also symbolize misguided ideas. Another popular symbol is the frog as a bearer of gold and silver, which if placed just inside the front door will attract wealth into the household.

Making Your Lily Pad and Frog

The lily pad is a very simple model, based upon a Japanese paper-cutting technique called *kirigami*. The leaf looks perfect when it is displayed alongside the frog and lotus flower. Use two squares of paper, equal in size. You will also need a pair of scissors.

1

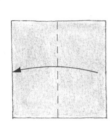

To make the lily pad:
Valley fold one square in half from right to left, with the coloured side on top.

2

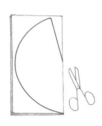

From the folded edge, cut out the lily pad shape as shown.

3

To complete the lily pad, unfold the paper.

7

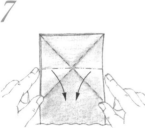

Bring the sides together and down towards you along the fold-lines made in steps 5 and 6.

8

Press the top down neatly into a triangle.

9

Valley fold the bottom edge up to meet the triangle's base.

4

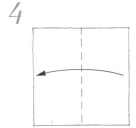

To make the frog:
Valley fold the remaining square in half from right to left, with the white side on top.

5

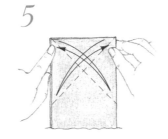

Fold and unfold the top part of the paper as shown.

6

Fold and unfold the top edge behind as shown.

10

Valley fold the sides in to meet the middle, leaving behind the top layers of the triangle.

11

Valley fold the bottom edge as shown. Valley fold the triangle's bottom points out from the middle, to make the front legs.

12

Valley fold the bottom flap's top corners down to meet the bottom edge.

13

Pinch both sides of the point and pull the outer layers apart, into the position shown in step 14. Press the paper flat.

14

Valley fold the two triangular flaps down.

15

Valley fold the flaps out from the middle, to make the frog's back legs.

16

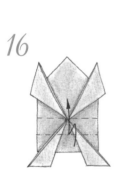

Step fold the bottom section of paper as shown.

17

The frog is finished. If you place him on a flat surface and press firmly on the base of his back, he will jump up into the air and may even turn a complete somersault.

Lotus Flower

In feng shui, the lotus flower is the symbol of triumph over adversity, hence it has gone on to symbolize spiritual evolution. Its roots in the mud represent the smaller or weaker forms of nature, the stem rising up through the water exemplifies intuition, and the flower blossoming in the sunlight depicts self-realization.

When placed in the northwest, the lotus flower inspires us to seek our fortune, whereas if placed in the southwest, it will help bickering partners to become united and fall in love all over again.

蓮華

蓮の花は精神の開花と成功、発展と富

31

Making Your Lotus Flower

Be very careful not to tear the paper when folding this pretty flower. If you make your lotus flower out of a starched cloth napkin, it will make a perfect table decoration. To begin with, practise with a white square of paper.

1

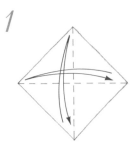

Crease the middle fold-lines as shown.

2

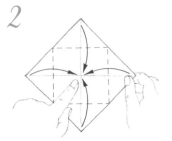

Valley fold the corners in to meet the middle, making a blintz base.

3

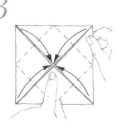

Again, valley fold the corners in to meet the middle.

7

From the top layer of paper, pull over a corner from behind. Stand the corner upright and shape it to look like a petal.

8

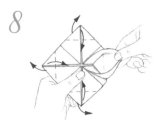

Repeat steps 6 and 7 with the remaining three corners, to make the first layer of petals.

9

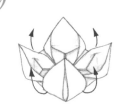

Pull over from behind the four corners from the next layer of paper, to make the second layer of petals.

4

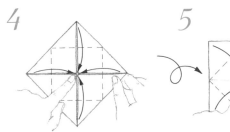

And again, valley fold the corners in to the middle. The result is three layers each comprising four corners.

5

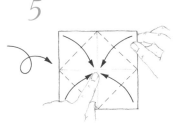

Turn the paper over. For the last time, valley fold the corners in to meet the middle.

6

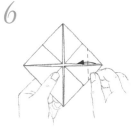

Valley fold over a little of one corner.

10

Pull over from behind the four corners from the final layer of paper, to make the third layer of petals.

11

The lotus flower is especially effective when combined with the lily pad and frog.

Crane

鶴

The crane is a symbol of longevity and wellbeing. Due to its long legs, which keep its body away from the mud, it also symbolizes purity. If placed in a northerly position in your chosen location, the crane will encourage positive career prospects, in the southeast it brings wealth, and in the south, fame and talent.

A book entitled *Senbazuru Orikata*, 'How to Fold a Thousand Cranes', was published in Japan in 1797, and in it the author, Gido Rokan, maintained the philosophy that if one crane represents a thousand years of happiness, then a hundred cranes equals one hundred thousand years of happiness, and a thousand cranes means one million years of happiness.

This most famous of origami models is used throughout the world as an object of peace.

鶴は長寿と無病息災を意味し
千年の幸福をもたらす

Making Your Crane

If you fold a thousand cranes within one year of your life and string them together, it is believed to confer longevity on you the creator, and to wish the recipient a long life and sustained good health. Use a square piece of paper, white side up.

1

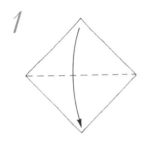

Turn the square around to look like a diamond. Valley fold it in half from top to bottom, to make a diaper fold.

2

Valley fold the paper in half from right to left.

3

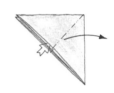

Lift the top layer up. Open out the paper and ...

4

... squash it down neatly into a diamond.

5

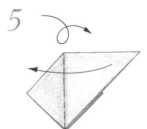

Turn the paper over. Repeat steps 2 to 4, to make a preliminary fold.

6

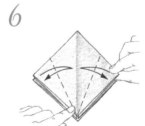

Fold and unfold the lower sloping edges (top half only) as shown.

7

Valley fold the top point down as shown.

8

Now, to make a petal fold, pinch and lift up the front flap of paper.

9

Continue to lift the flap up until its edges meet along the middle line.

13

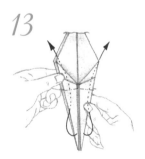

Inside reverse fold the bottom points.

14

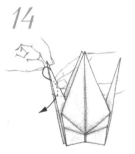

Inside reverse fold the tip of one of the points, to make the crane's head and beak.

15

Fold the wings down slightly.

10

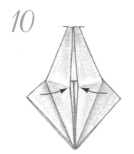

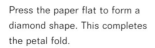

Press the paper flat to form a diamond shape. This completes the petal fold.

11

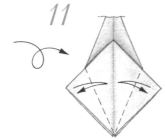

Turn the paper over. Repeat steps 6 to 10, to make a bird base.

12

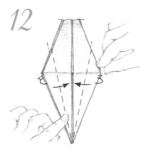

Valley fold the lower sloping edges (top layer only), so they lie along the middle line. Turn the paper over and repeat.

16

Holding the wings as shown, gently pull them apart in order to flatten out the middle point a little.

17

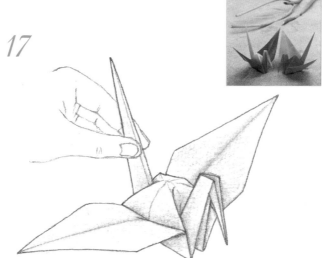

The completed crane.

CHINESE HOROSCOPE ANIMALS

干支を折る

The Chinese lunar calendar follows the cycle of the moon, and is formed differently to the Western solar calendar. In the Chinese calendar, the beginning of the year falls somewhere between late January and early February. The Chinese adopted the Western calendar in 1911, but the lunar calendar is still used for Chinese New Year and other festive occasions.

The Chinese horoscope revolves around twelve animals. Each year is represented by an animal, so each cycle lasts for twelve years, beginning with the rat and ending with the pig. Each animal has set characteristics which, it is said, are present in people born within that particular year.

Note: The Tiger and Dragon are Guardians as well as Chinese Horoscope Animals. Their folding instructions can be found on pages 87 and 92 respectively.

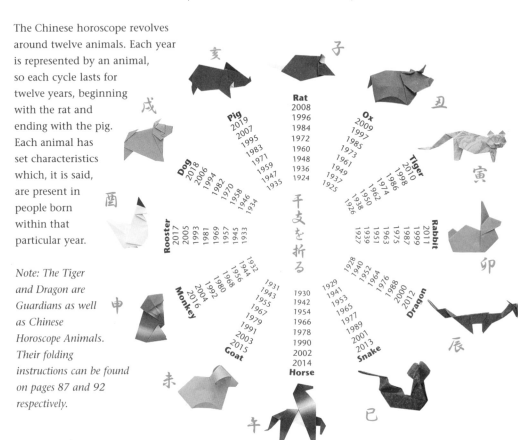

亥

子

戌

丑

Pig
2019
2007
1995
1983
1971
1959
1947
1935

Rat
2008
1996
1984
1972
1960
1948
1936
1924

Ox
2009
1997
1985
1973
1961
1949
1937
1925

寅

Dog
2018
2006
1994
1982
1970
1958
1946
1934

Tiger
2010
1998
1986
1974
1962
1950
1938
1926

酉

Rooster
2017
2005
1993
1981
1969
1957
1945
1933

干支を折る

Rabbit
2011
1999
1987
1975
1963
1951
1939
1927

卯

Monkey
2004
1992
1980
1968
1956
1944
1932

1931
1943
1955
1967
1979
1991
2003
2015

1930
1942
1954
1966
1978
1990
2002
2014

1928
1940
1952
1964
1976
1988
2000
2012

1929
1941
1953
1965
1977
1989
2001
2013

Dragon

辰

申

Goat

未

Horse

午

Snake

巳

The Rat

People born in the Year of the Rat are renowned for their charm. Although easily angered, they appear to be cool, calm and completely under control. Rat people are very likeable and have a great deal of ambition and integrity. They like to live well, are good to themselves and love to gossip. Naturally thrifty, they are good at saving money (and can be stingy too). They are successful in businesses where they are in contact with people or if a creative activity, such as writing, is involved. Being in love brings out their generous side, but they have a tendency not to realize if their love isn't being reciprocated. They are most compatible with those born in the years of the Dragon and the Ox.

子―鼠

子年の人は人
且つ野心

Making Your Rat

To enhance the finished result, try to use paper that matches a rat's appearance. Use a square piece of paper, coloured side up.

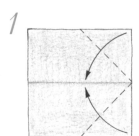

Crease the middle fold-line as shown. Valley fold the right-hand corners in to meet the middle fold-line.

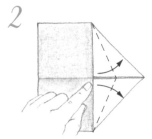

Valley fold the corners as shown.

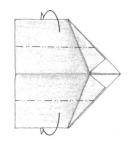

Mountain fold the top and bottom edges to meet the middle fold-line.

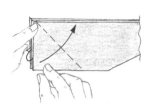

Valley fold the bottom left-hand corner (top layer only) up to meet the top edge. Repeat behind.

Inside reverse fold the hidden point upwards, to make an ear. Repeat behind.

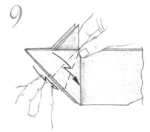

Step fold the left-hand point on either side as shown, to make the head.

4

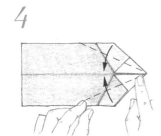

From the right-hand point, valley fold the sloping edges in to meet the middle fold-line.

5

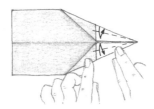

Again from the right-hand point, fold and unfold the sloping edges in to the middle fold-line. Crease them only as far as shown.

6

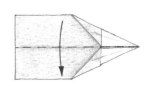

Valley fold the paper in half from top to bottom.

10

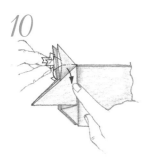

Open out an ear and squash it down neatly. Repeat with the other ear.

11

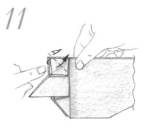

Then open the ears out to make them three-dimensional.

12

Shape the rat's underside with a mountain fold on each side.

13

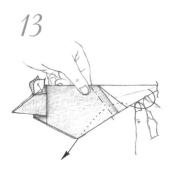

Inside reverse fold the right-hand point down inside the model and …

14

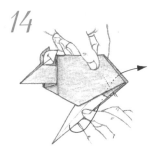

… back out as shown, to make the tail.

15

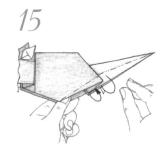

Narrow down the tail with a mountain fold on each side. These folds take place along the fold-lines made in step 5.

16

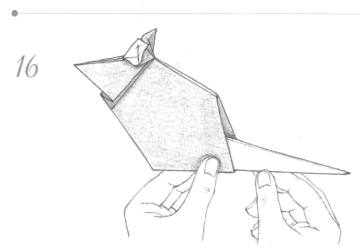

The completed rat.

The Ox

The Year of the Ox produces people that, like their sign, are placid and easy-going. They can, however, become stubborn and angry if forced to act against their will. They have the rare gift of inspiring others, and their self-assuredness can help them become successful. Ox people can be very creative with their hands. They are naturally quiet although they can produce great eloquence if required to speak in public. Their shrewdness and reliability makes them very good at doing business. Although they are often misunderstood because of their cool attitudes and unemotional responses, they make faithful, loving and devoted partners. They are most compatible with Snake, Rooster and Rat people.

丑一牛

Making Your Ox

The folds in steps 6, 7 and 11 can prove tricky, but with a little patience they will fall into place. Use a square piece of paper, white side up.

1

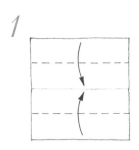

Crease the middle fold-line as shown. Valley fold the top and bottom edges in to meet the middle fold-line.

2

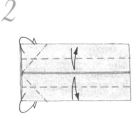

Fold and unfold the top and bottom edges. Mountain fold the left-hand corners behind to meet the middle fold-line.

3

Valley fold the left-hand point.

7

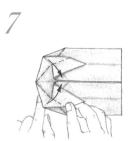

... and fold the flaps along the middle fold-line, as shown in step 8. This makes the ox's horns.

8

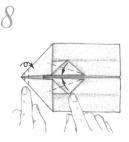

Valley fold each horn in half. Fold over and over a little of the left-hand point twice, to make the ox's snout.

9

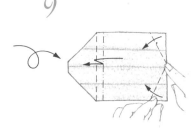

Turn the paper over. Step fold the left-hand section as shown. Valley fold both right-hand corners to meet their adjacent fold-lines, so they form a point.

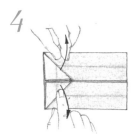

4

Pinch the point's outer layers and pull them apart, into the position shown in step 5. Press them flat to make two triangular flaps.

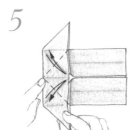

5

Fold and unfold the flaps as shown.

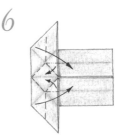

6

Carefully fold the flaps along the creases made in the previous step, while folding the two middle triangles up into the diamond …

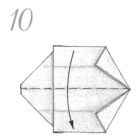

10

Valley fold the paper in half from top to bottom.

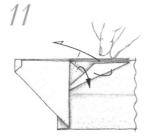

11

Mountain fold a horn upwards, and at the same time release the triangular section from inside the horn, as shown, to make an ear. Repeat behind.

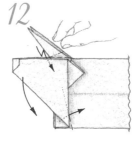

12

Step fold the horns down inside the model. Pull the snout downwards slightly. Press it flat, into the position shown in step 13. This makes the ox's head.

13

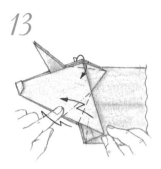

Valley fold the head's top point slightly. Repeat behind. Step fold the neck into place on either side, as shown.

14

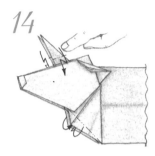

Shape a horn with a step fold. Mountain fold a little of the neck inside the model. Repeat both procedures behind.

15

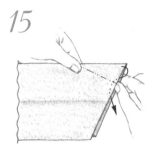

Inside reverse fold a little of the right-hand point downwards, to make the ox's tail.

16

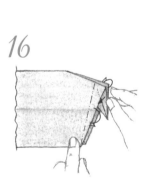

Valley fold the tail's top layer in half, while at the same time pushing the triangular area inwards as shown by the mountain fold-line. Repeat behind.

17

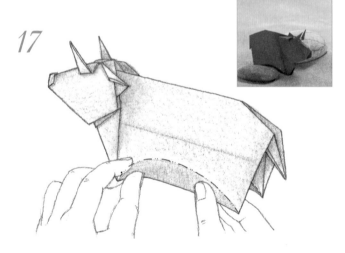

To complete the ox, mountain fold the bottom edges inwards slightly.

The Rabbit

People who are born in the Year of the Rabbit are gifted, ambitious and very smooth talkers. They are respectable and trustworthy and are renowned for their good taste. Rabbit people like to avoid confrontation wherever possible, but show bravery against high odds. They like their lives to be peaceful and calm, and value security and comfort. They're lucky financially, with an uncanny ability to pick a winner. However, where money matters are concerned, they usually think things over very carefully and never back out of a contract.

They can be affectionate, but would rather be alone than in an unsatisfactory relationship. They are likely to form successful relationships with people born in the years of the Goat, the Pig and the Dog.

卯年の人は平穏を好む
人から信頼される

卯―兎

Making Your Rabbit

In the world of origami, animals can be particularly challenging. Once you have folded an animal, slight variations can be introduced to change its overall shape and form. Use a square piece of paper, white side up.

1

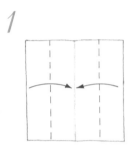

Crease the middle fold-line as shown. Valley fold the sides in to meet the middle fold-line.

2

Fold and unfold the paper in half from bottom to top.

3

Fold and unfold the top corners as shown.

7

Pinch together the same edges along the fold-lines made in step 6, while mountain folding the paper in half. A flap will appear.

8

Mountain fold the right-hand top layer of paper on a line between the top point and the fold-line made in step 2. Repeat behind.

9

Fold and unfold the paper as shown.

4

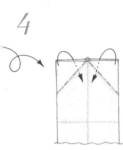

Turn the paper over. Inside reverse fold the corners along the fold-lines made in step 3.

5

Fold and unfold the top point as shown.

6

Fold and unfold the point's sloping edges down to meet the fold-line made in step 5.

10

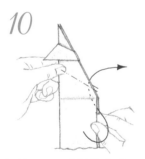

Inside reverse fold the bottom section up to the right along the fold-lines made in step 9.

11

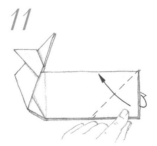

Valley fold the bottom right-hand corner (top layer only) up to meet the top edge. Repeat behind.

12

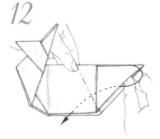

Inside reverse fold the right-hand point into the position shown in step 13.

13

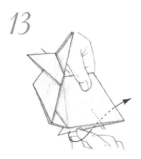

Reverse fold the point back out, to make the rabbit's tail.

14

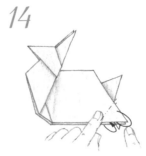

Shape the base of the tail with a mountain fold. Repeat behind.

15

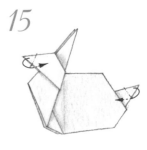

Blunt the rabbit's nose and tail with inside reverse folds.

16

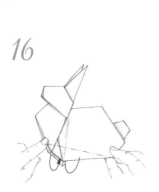

Shape the rabbit's underside with a mountain fold on each side.

17

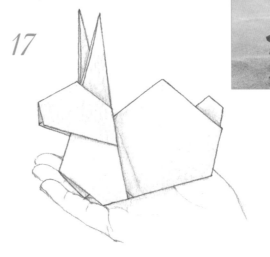

The finished rabbit.

The Snake

People born in the Year of the Snake are endowed with tremendous wisdom. Deep thinkers, they prefer to rely on their intellect rather than trust the judgement of others. They are fired with intense determination and hate to fail at anything. They can annoy the people around them with their tendency to overdo whatever they undertake, even if they are trying to help others. They seldom have money worries as they are usually rich, yet they do have a stingy side, and hate to lend people money. Snake people have very good taste but tend to be vain. They can be very jealous and possessive in their relationships. They are most compatible with people born in the years of the Ox and the Rooster.

已 ー 蛇

已年の人は賢明で失敗をせぬ

Making Your Snake

The folding of this particular model is based around the reverse fold. It may appear difficult at first but should become easier with practice. Use a square piece of paper, white side up.

1

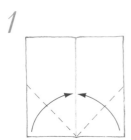

Crease the middle fold-line as shown. Valley fold the bottom corners in to meet the middle fold-line

2

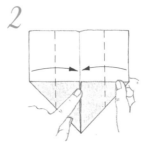

Valley fold the sides in to meet the middle fold-line.

3

Fold and unfold the sides as shown. Mountain fold the paper in half from top to bottom.

7

Open out the layers slightly as shown and ...

8

... push the middle ridge down as shown by the valley fold. Mountain fold both sides and flatten them into the position shown in step 9.

9

Inside reverse fold the flattened section of paper up and ...

4

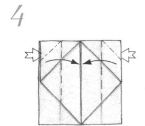

Valley fold the front flap's sides in to meet the middle line and, as you do so ...

5

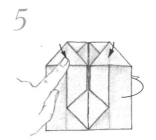

... squash down their top corners into triangles as shown. Mountain fold the paper in half from right to left.

6

Inside reverse fold the top right-hand corner.

10

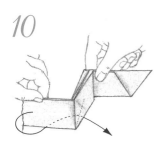

... down as shown.

11

Inside reverse fold the section's middle ridge of paper, to make the snake's head.

12

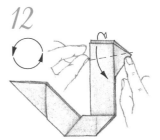

Turn the paper around into the position shown. Valley fold the head's front layer of paper. Repeat behind.

13

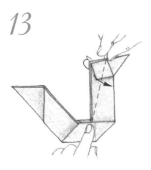

Valley fold the front layer of paper as shown. Repeat behind.

14

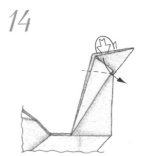

Outside reverse fold the snake's head.

15

Valley fold the head over towards the left a little.

16

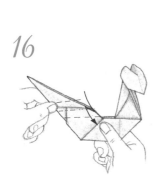

Step fold the tail into place.

17

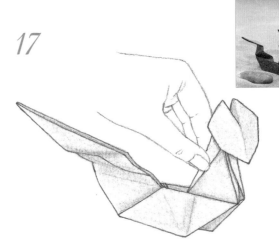

Open the base out slightly to complete the snake.

The Horse

People born in the Year of the Horse are popular and cheerful. They love to compliment others, but tend to act before they think, and have short tempers. Fired with intense strength and inspirational confidence, horse people are quick witted, talented, hard-working and enjoy large crowds and entertainment. They are perfectionists, are good with their hands and are usually good at managing their finances. They are perceptive, although they sometimes talk too much. And due to their independent nature, they often refuse to listen to advice. Generally well groomed and passionate in love, they can be maddeningly indifferent in other situations. They are most compatible with people born in the years of the Tiger, the Dog and the Goat.

午年の人は完全主義者だが時に考えより行動が先走る

午－馬

Making Your Horse

*W*ith this model, try to make your cuts and folds as neat and accurate as possible. Use a square piece of paper, white side up. You will also need a pair of scissors.

1

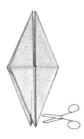

Follow steps 1 to 11 of the crane (*see pages 35–7*). Taking the half that is joined down the middle, cut one layer at a time, being careful not to slit the middle point.

2

Step fold a lower right-hand flap as shown, to make a back leg. Repeat behind.

3

Inside reverse fold the top right-hand point down.

7

Blunt the horse's legs with inside reverse folds.

8

Inside reverse fold the top point, to make the head.

9

Blunt the snout with an inside reverse fold.

4

Inside reverse fold the point back up into the position shown in step 5, to make the tail.

5

Shape the top of a back leg with a mountain fold. Repeat behind.

6

Valley fold the tail as shown.

10

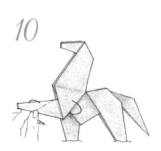

Mountain fold a front leg up, and then down, to suggest movement.

11

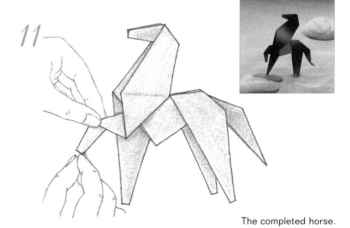

The completed horse.

The Goat

People born in the Year of the Goat are true artists and are highly elegant. They are happiest when they are being creative. On the negative side, Goat people are pessimistic, puzzled by life and seem to lack a sense of direction. They are usually deeply religious and have a timid nature. They are ideas people, but lack the determination to carry out their ideas alone. If money isn't an issue, they prefer to do voluntary work for a charity, rather than earn a living. However, they prefer not to brag about their charitable side. Because of their basic insecurity, Goat people need guidance from those around them. They have a passionate, wise and gentle nature. They connect most successfully with people born in the years of the Rabbit, the Pig and the Horse.

未年の人は洗練された芸術周りの助けを必要と

Making Your Goat

With just a few folds you can make a goat with a set of magnificent horns. Use a square piece of paper, white side up.

1

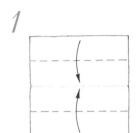

Crease the middle fold-line as shown. Valley fold the top and bottom edges to meet the middle fold-line.

2

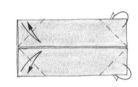

Fold and unfold the left-hand corners as shown. Mountain fold the right-hand corners behind to meet the middle fold-line.

3

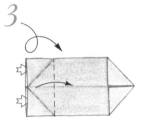

Turn the paper over. Open out the left-hand layers along the fold-lines made in step 2.

4

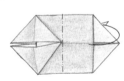

Flatten them down neatly into two triangles. Mountain fold the paper in half from right to left.

5

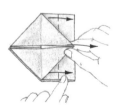

Pull the triangles over towards the right, to make a valley fold as shown.

6

Mountain fold the paper in half from top to bottom.

7

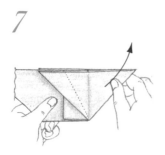

Pull the right-hand point upwards as far as the paper will allow you. Press the paper flat into the position shown in step 8.

8

Step fold the right-hand point on either side down into the model.

9

Fold the triangular flap over, as though turning the page of a book. Repeat behind.

13

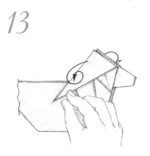

Shape the horns by curling them.

14

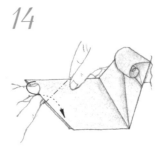

Inside reverse fold the left-hand point down inside the model.

15

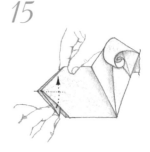

Valley fold the reversed point up inside the model, so closing up the goat's back.

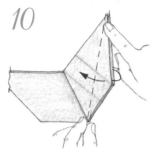

10

Valley fold the flap's side point (top layer only) on a line between the top and bottom points, to make a horn. Repeat behind.

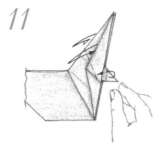

11

Fold and unfold the horns as shown. Blunt the protruding point on the right-hand side with an inside reverse fold, to make the goat's snout.

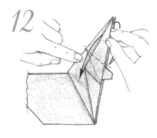

12

Valley fold the horns on either side of the model, as shown.

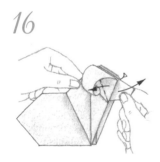

16

Pull the snout up a little along the fold-lines made in step 11, to make the horns rise up.

17

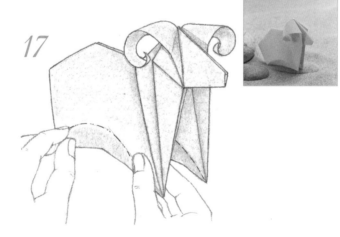

To complete the goat, mountain fold the bottom edges inwards slightly.

The Monkey

People born in the Year of the Monkey tend to achieve success in any field they choose. They read a great deal and have extremely good memories, so they are unusually well informed. If they follow their natural path, monkey people are likely to become famous in some way. They are inclined to back away from fights and arguments. They are able to make decisions easily, are good at making deals, and are skilful in business diplomacy.

申－猿

申年の人は記憶力に優れ

Monkey people have a lot of common sense, although they do have a tendency to look down on others. They often talk too much, driving friends away with their lengthy explanations and endless chatter. They are most compatible with people born in the years of the Dragon and the Rat.

Making Your Monkey

Try changing the angle of the folds in step 7 each time you make this model, to see how many different expressions you can give your monkeys. Use a square piece of paper, white side up.

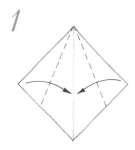

1

Crease the middle fold-line as shown. From the top point, valley fold the edges in to the middle fold-line, to make a kite base.

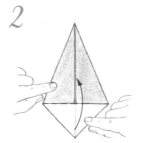

2

Valley fold the bottom point up on a line between the two side points.

3

Valley fold the paper in half from right to left.

4

Valley fold the bottom left-hand point to meet the opposite edge, as shown. Repeat behind.

5

Turn the paper around a little. Valley fold the left-hand edges over as far as shown.

6

Open out the point and squash it down neatly into the position shown in step 7, to make the monkey's face.

7

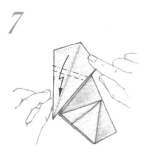

Shape the face with a step fold as shown.

8

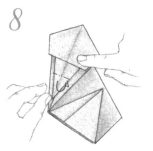

Mountain fold the tip of the face, up inside the model.

9

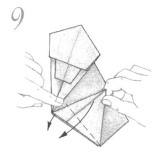

Valley fold the front point down, to make a leg. Repeat behind.

10

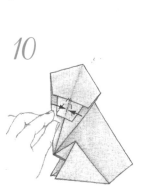

Pinch the monkey's nose into shape.

11

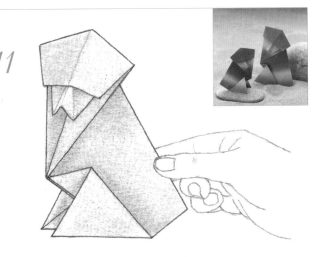

Your monkey is complete.

The Rooster

The Year of the Rooster breeds busybodies, deep thinkers and eccentrics. They are often brilliant at everything they do, practical, and a source of intrigue to others. Always positive-minded, they have confidence in their own beliefs and actions. Shyness isn't a problem for Rooster people – they speak out boldly when they have something to say. But they are inclined to be selfish and can forget to consider others. Devoted to their work, they do have a tendency to steam ahead with challenges that are destined to fail. But luckily, Rooster people have wonderful powers of recovery and frequently strut their way through difficult situations. They best relate to people born in the years of the Ox, the Dragon and the Snake.

酉年の人は周囲の注目を浴びる自信家

酉ー鶏

Making Your Rooster

Steps 8, 13 and 14 of this model are a bit tricky, so do take your time folding them. Use a square piece of paper, coloured side up

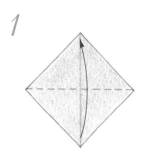

Crease the middle fold-line as shown. Valley fold the paper in half from bottom to top.

Fold and unfold the top point (upper layer only) as shown.

Fold and unfold the top point's sloping edges (upper layer only) to meet the fold-line made in step 2.

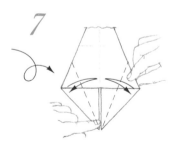

Turn the paper over. From the bottom point, fold and unfold the sloping edges in to meet the middle line.

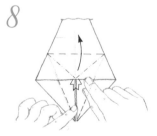

Pinch and lift the horizontal edge, so that the sloping edges fold in along the fold-lines made in step 7, and meet the middle line.

Press the paper down neatly to make a triangular flap. Valley fold the flap down as far as it will go.

4

Pinch the point's sloping edges together along the fold-lines made in step 3. Valley fold the small triangular flap that appears to the left, to make the rooster's comb.

5

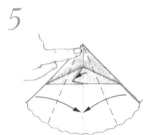

From the top point, valley fold the sloping edges in to meet the middle fold-line. The rooster's comb should remain visible.

6

Fold and unfold the top point down to meet the horizontal edge that is currently hidden at the back of the model.

10

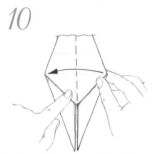

Valley fold the paper in half from right to left.

11

Step fold the top point on either side, as shown, to make the rooster's head.

12

Step fold the head on either side as shown, to make the beak.

13

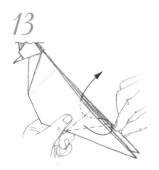

Inside reverse fold a bottom
point upwards, while at the
same time opening it out into
the position shown in step 14.

14

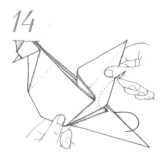

Repeat step 13 with the other
bottom point, to produce tail
feathers.

15

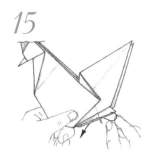

Inside reverse fold the triangular
flap to the left, to make the feet.

16

The finished rooster.

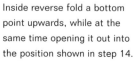

The Dog

People born in the Year of the Dog are blessed with most of the finer traits of human nature. Just like man's best friend, they are loyal, with a far-reaching sense of duty. You can trust a Dog person to keep a secret, hence they are held in high regard by others. They are renowned for championing good causes, as they cannot stand injustice, and they have good business sense which inspires confidence, but they frequently find fault with others and cannot tolerate sarcasm. Dog people are warm, kind and generous but their compassion for others sometimes turns to endless worry. They dislike small talk and refuse to take part in it. Like Rooster people, they can be selfish, eccentric and obstinate. They are most compatible with people born in the years of the Goat, the Horse and the Dragon.

戌―犬

Making Your Dog

*M*any types of dog can evolve from the diamond base. Try experimenting with folding techniques that are similar to each other, such as step folds and reverse folds, to invent your own origami dog. Use a square piece of paper, white side up.

1

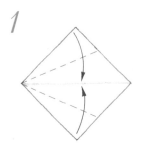

Crease the middle fold-line as shown. From the left-hand point, valley fold the edges in to meet the fold-line, making a kite base.

2

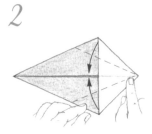

From the right-hand point, valley fold the sloping edges in to meet the middle fold-line, to make a diamond base.

3

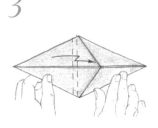

Step fold the left-hand point as shown.

7

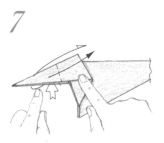

Once again, outside reverse fold the point, to make the dog's head.

8

Step fold the head on either side as shown.

9

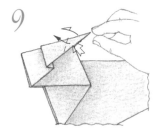

Outside reverse fold the head's tip, to suggest the dog's ears.

4

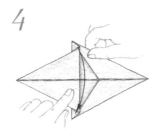

Valley fold the paper in half from top to bottom.

5

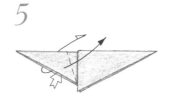

Outside reverse fold the left-hand point into the position shown in step 6.

6

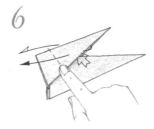

Again, outside reverse fold the point, so it points to the left.

10

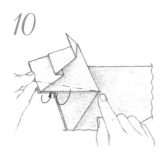

Shape the head with a mountain fold. Repeat behind.

11

Valley fold the neck's top layer in half, while pushing the triangular area inwards as shown by the mountain fold-line. Repeat behind.

12

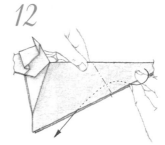

Inside reverse fold the right-hand point into the position shown in step 13.

13

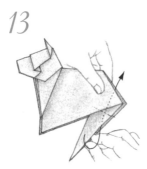

Reverse fold the point back out again, to make the dog's hind legs and tail.

14

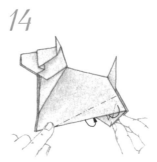

On a line from the base of the tail to the step fold, mountain fold the bottom edges while narrowing the hind legs with a valley fold.

15

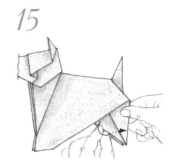

Inside reverse fold the triangular section of paper between the hind legs, as shown, to separate them slightly.

16

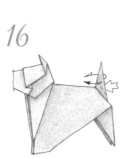

Outside reverse fold the tail's tip.

17

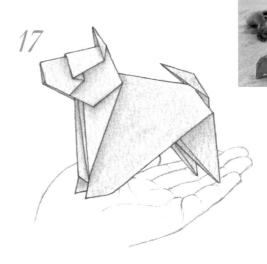

The completed dog.

The Pig

People born in the Year of the Pig are wonderfully trustworthy, obliging and gallant. They have tremendous inner strength and are likely to be successful at whatever they undertake. They are also well informed and highly intelligent. Pig people aren't indecisive, but they do tend to be slow decision makers. Despite their general easy-going nature, they can be very determined and always realize their ambitions, preferring to solve all their problems alone rather than seeking help. They treat their loved ones with great kindness, creating peaceful and happy relationships. Although they have very few friends, the ones they make they intend to keep for life and will be extremely loyal to. They are most compatible with people born in the Year of the Goat.

亥－猪

亥年の人は忠誠心と
自立心に富む

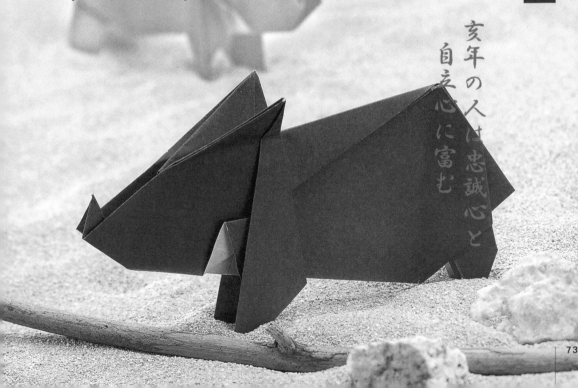

Making Your Pig

If you use a few folds to form just main features, you can create a model that is simple yet clearly resembles a particular object. This pig is a perfect example of that technique. Use a square piece of paper, white side up.

1

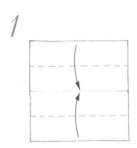

Crease the middle fold-line as shown. Valley fold the top and bottom edges to meet the middle fold-line.

2

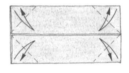

Fold and unfold the corners as shown.

3

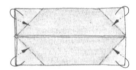

Inside reverse fold the corners along the fold-lines made in step 2, to make four points.

7

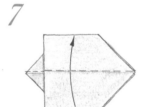

Valley fold the paper in half from bottom to top.

8

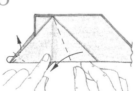

Inside reverse fold the left-hand point making the snout. Valley fold the triangle to make a front leg, as shown in step 9. Repeat behind.

9

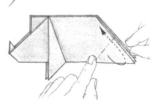

Taking the top layer only, mountain fold the bottom right-hand point up …

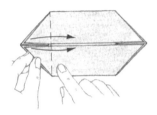

Valley fold the two left-hand points over to the right, revealing a triangle shape underneath.

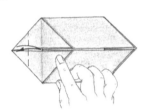

Fold and unfold this triangle, as shown.

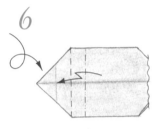

Turn the paper over. Step fold the left-hand section using the fold-line from step 5 as a guide. Don't fold the flaps that are underneath.

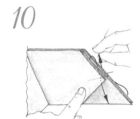

... and back down into the position shown in step 11. Turn the pig over and repeat steps 9 and 10. This makes the back legs.

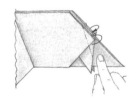

Shape the back legs with a mountain fold on each side.

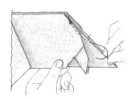

Inside reverse fold the remaining right-hand point up inside the model, to make the tail.

13

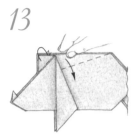

Shape the pig's back with a valley fold as shown, while at the same time squashing down the adjoining point.

14

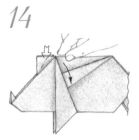

Repeat step 13 with the remaining flap, but valley fold over the previous fold as shown, to close up the pig's back.

15

Release a little of the paper adjacent to the front leg and step fold it as shown, to suggest a tusk. Repeat behind.

16

Valley fold the two top points down slightly to make the ears.

17

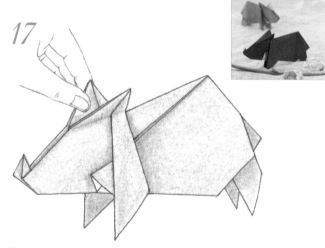

Your pig is finished.

THE FOUR GUARDIANS

The most elementary of directions are the points of the compass: North, South, East and West. Feng shui associates these directions with symbolic animal spirits, collectively known as the Four Guardians. These are shown here.

According to the ancient principles of feng shui, the positioning of a home in relation to its surroundings can affect the prosperity and wellbeing of those who live there. The high and low structures around the home, such as buildings, hills and ponds symbolize the four guardians.

玄武

Tortoise
Colour: Black
Ruling direction: North

白虎

Tiger
Colour: White
Ruling direction: West

Dragon
Colour: Green
Ruling direction: East

青龍

Phoenix
Colour: Red
Ruling direction: South

朱雀

In today's modern high-rise society, it's almost impossible to put into place the ancient practices of feng shui where property location is concerned. However, we can use the directional attributes of the four guardians to encourage an auspicious flow of chi into the home, thus restoring happiness and improving quality of life. Ideally, the guardians should be placed in a room that is used by the whole family and where they spend the most time together. An image of a tortoise – whether it be an ornament, a picture or other form – should be positioned in the north of the room, a phoenix in the south, a dragon in the east and a tiger in the west. When positioning the dragon and the tiger, ensure that they are directly opposite each other and that their tails are pointing towards the north.

四神の靈力

The Red Phoenix

This mythical creature is said to live for five hundred years, at the close of which it makes a nest, flaps its wings to start a fire, burns itself to ashes and rises again to live another cycle. In feng shui, the red phoenix represents the female, and presides over the southern quadrant of the heavens where it symbolizes sun, warmth, summer and harvest. In the surroundings of the home, the influence of the red phoenix is carried through the presence of a low hill or, in built-up areas, a low wall.

朱雀―不死鳥

赤い不死鳥は南の守護神
女性を象徴する

Making Your Red Phoenix

This model can at first appear quite difficult. But if you study each illustration carefully to make sure you are following the instructions correctly, making the phoenix will soon become easier. Use a square piece of red paper, white side up.

1

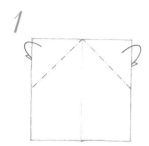

Crease the middle fold-line as shown. Mountain fold the top corners behind to meet the middle fold-line.

2

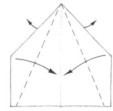

From the top point, valley fold the sloping edges in to meet the middle fold-line, while …

3

… letting the corners from underneath flick up.

4

Turn the paper over. From the top point, valley fold the sloping edges in to meet the middle fold-line.

5

Starting just below the top point, valley fold the sloping edges over towards the middle fold-line.

6

Mountain fold the top point on a line between the two side points.

7

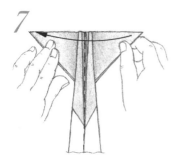

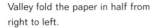

Valley fold the paper in half from right to left.

8

Lift the left-hand point up. Open it out and squash it down neatly into a diamond. Repeat behind, to make a preliminary fold.

9

Follow steps 6 to 11 of the crane (see pages 35–7) to make a bird base.

13

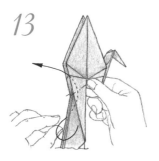

Inside reverse fold the left-hand section of paper into the position shown in step 14, to make the phoenix's tail.

14

Gently pull the wings apart, to flatten the middle point out a little.

15

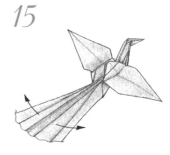

Open out the tail slightly.

10

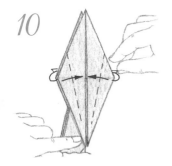

Valley fold the lower sloping edges over, so they lie along the middle line. Repeat behind.

11

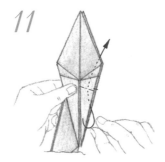

Inside reverse fold the bottom right-hand point into the position shown in step 12.

12

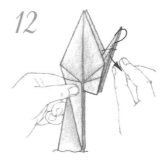

Inside reverse fold the point's tip, to make the head and beak.

16

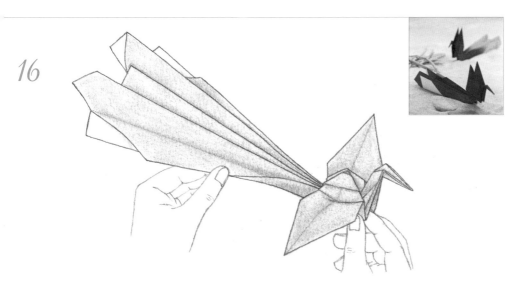

This completes the red phoenix.

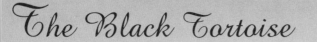

The Black Tortoise

In Chinese folklore, the tortoise supports the world, its four feet representing the four corners of the Earth. The black tortoise, which is said to live for ten thousand years, is a symbol of longevity, strength, indestructibility and prosperity. Hills, trees or high buildings in the north, behind your house are, according to the principles of feng shui, said to protect the home and its inhabitants, like a tortoise's shell.

玄武ー黒い亀

亀は世界を支え万年の命を持つ

Making Your Black Tortoise

The black tortoise model is very popular among Japanese children, but is comparatively unknown in the West. Use a square piece of black paper, white side up.

1

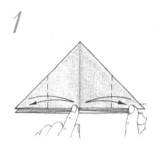

Follow steps 1 to 6 of the goldfish (*see page 21*) to make a waterbomb base. Fold and unfold the bottom points (top two layers only) as shown.

2

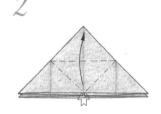

Valley fold the top layer of paper in half from bottom to top …

3

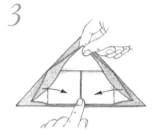

… making the bottom points rise up. Fold the edges in …

4

… so they meet along the middle line.

5

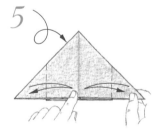

Turn the paper over. Fold and unfold the bottom points as shown. Repeat steps 2 to 4.

6

Valley fold the top point in to the middle.

7

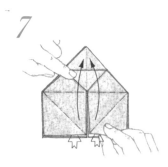

Open up the two square layers at the bottom and …

8

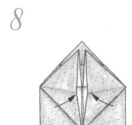

… squash them neatly into triangle shapes.

9

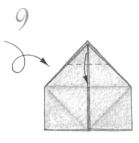

Turn the paper over. Repeat steps 6 to 8.

13

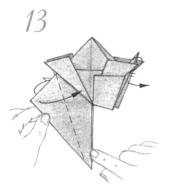

Inside reverse fold the point's tip, to make the tail. Valley fold the left-hand sloping edge, as shown. Repeat behind.

14

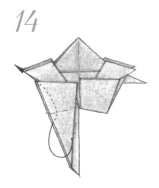

Inside reverse fold the bottom left-hand point, to make the tortoise's neck.

15

Gently pull the legs apart while flattening out the middle point a little, so the tortoise becomes three-dimensional.

10

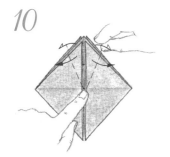

Valley fold the top points out from the middle, as shown, to make two of the legs. Repeat behind.

11

From the bottom point, valley fold the right-hand sloping edge over, so that it lies along the middle line. Repeat behind.

12

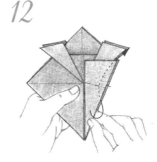

Inside reverse fold the bottom right-hand point.

16

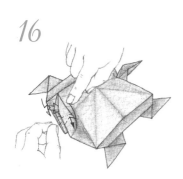

Step fold the neck on either side, as shown, to make the tortoise's head.

17

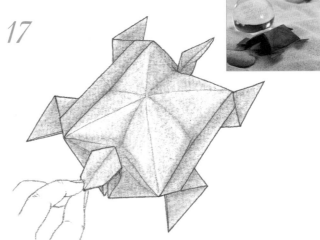

The completed black tortoise.

The White Tiger

The Guardian

In Asia, the tiger is considered to be the king of the wild animals and, hence is seen as the natural symbol for royalty, power and fearlessness. It is also believed that the tiger's image will drive away any evil spirits. The tiger represents yin energy, which is female. The white tiger and the green dragon are said to guard the site of the home. They are symbolized by lower structures than the black tortoise, such as low hills or slopes.

The Horoscope Animal

People born in the Year of the Tiger are powerful, courageous and philosophical. They are respected by others, which can lead them to become rulers of some kind. Tiger people find decision making hard. They are suspicious and narrow-minded and although they have great respect for their elders and those in authority, they tend to resent them. They can be stubborn, selfish and mean with money, but deep down they are sensitive and loving. Tiger people are usually lucky enough in life to escape serious problems. They are most compatible with people born in the years of the Horse and the Dragon.

寅年の人は意志強固
勇敢で冷静な賢者

虎はその勇姿で
鬼気を払い除ける

Making Your White Tiger

*T*he procedure involving two pieces of origami that are joined together to make one model is called compound origami. This technique is very useful for making animals. Use two squares of white paper equal in size. You will also need a pair of scissors and some glue.

1

HEAD

Cut one piece to the size shown and set aside. Fold the other into a bird base, following steps 1 to 11 of the crane (*see pages 35–7*).

2

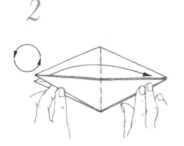

To make the body: Turn the bird base so the half that is joined down the middle points left. Valley fold the top flap from left to right.

3

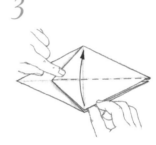

Valley fold the bottom point up (top layer only).

4

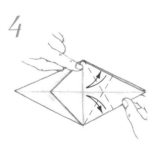

Fold and unfold the top right-hand flap as shown.

5

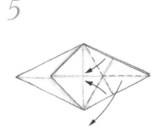

Pinch the flap's sloping edges together along the existing fold-lines, to make a point, as shown.

6

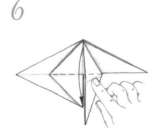

Flatten the point downwards. Take the point at the top, and valley fold the upper two layers down.

7

Repeat steps 4 and 5, but this time ...

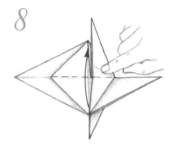

8

... flatten the point upwards. Valley fold the bottom point up (top layer only).

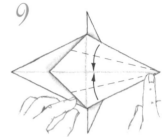

9

From the right-hand point, valley fold the sloping edges in to meet the middle fold-line.

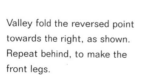

13

Valley fold the reversed point towards the right, as shown. Repeat behind, to make the front legs.

14

Blunt the front legs with an inside reverse fold. Give the right-hand point one or two inside reverse folds to create the tail. This completes the body.

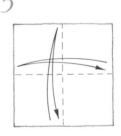

15

To make the head: Take the smaller square that you prepared in step 1 and crease the middle fold-lines as shown.

10

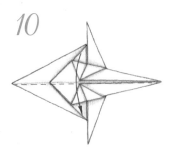

Valley fold the whole model in half from top to bottom. There should now be two triangles pointing downwards.

11

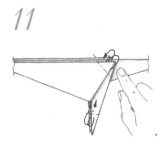

Blunt the tips of these triangles with an inside reverse fold, to make the back legs. Mountain fold the tops of the back legs to shape them.

12

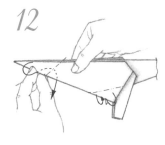

Inside reverse fold the left-hand point. Shape the tiger's underside with a mountain fold. Repeat behind.

16

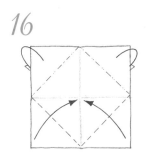

Mountain fold the top corners, and valley fold the bottom corners, in to the middle.

17

From the top point, valley fold the sloping edges in to meet the middle fold-line, while letting the corners from underneath flick up.

18

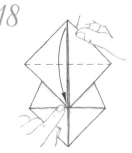

Valley fold the top point down on a line between the two side points.

19

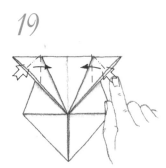

Open out each side point and squash them down neatly into diamonds.

20

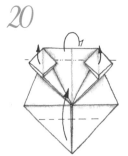

Mountain fold the top edge while folding back the top layer of each diamond, to make the ears. Valley fold the bottom flap up …

21

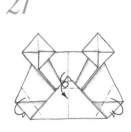

… and fold its tip over and over to make the nose. To complete the head, shape its sides with mountain folds.

22

To assemble: Glue the head on to the body at the desired angle.

23

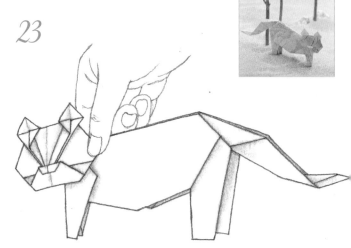

Your finished white tiger.

The Green Dragon

The Guardian

The dragon, the most beloved and celebrated creature in Chinese mythology, is considered one of the foremost symbols of strength, goodness, courage and endurance. It is also the emblem of vigilance and security, and the spirit of change. The dragon represents yang energy, which is male. The pairing of the green dragon with the white tiger is an important feng shui principle, for when the two merge, the most auspicious chi is created.

The Horoscope Animal

The Year of the Dragon breeds people born with the gifts of health, energy, courage and sensitivity, who often succeed in the tasks they undertake. It is said that they are blessed with virtue, riches, harmony and longevity. Dragon people are sincere and never borrow money. They are capable of great success as well as spectacular failure, and are susceptible to flattery. They make good workers but at times display a willingness to work for negative purposes. People born in the Year of the Dragon are quick tempered, excitable and enormously stubborn. They often bypass marriage only to face loneliness in their old age. They are most compatible with people born in the years of the Rat, Snake and Monkey.

青龍—緑の龍

龍は中国伝説の中で最も重要で名高い架空の動物

辰年の人は健康で精力的勇敢で且つ繊細

Making Your Green Dragon

This compound origami model is made up of two similar units, so be very careful not to mix up your paper or the folding steps. Use two squares of green paper equal in size. You will also need some glue.

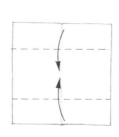

To make the front half: Taking one square white side up, crease the middle fold-line. Valley fold the top and bottom edges to meet it.

Fold and unfold the right- and left-hand corners as shown.

Inside reverse fold the corners along the fold-lines made in step 2.

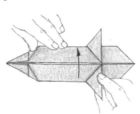

Valley fold the paper in half from bottom to top.

Outside reverse fold the left-hand point, to make the dragon's head.

Inside reverse fold the two points that are hidden inside the front of the head, to make the dragon's horns.

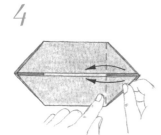

4

Valley fold the right-hand points (top layer only) over to the left.

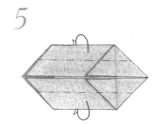

5

Mountain fold the top and bottom edges behind to meet the middle fold-line.

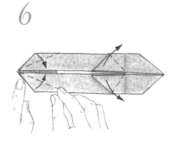

6

From the left-hand point, valley fold the corners in to the middle fold-line. Valley fold the right-hand points outwards as shown.

10

Valley fold the horns out to either side. Shape the snout with an outside reverse fold.

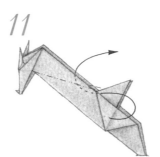

11

Inside reverse fold the lower section of paper up to the right.

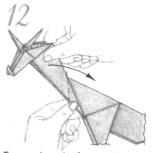

12

To complete the front half of your dragon, valley fold the head over towards the right.

13

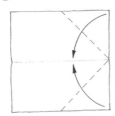

To make the back half: Taking the second square white side up, crease the middle fold-line. Valley fold the right-hand corners.

14

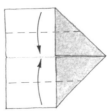

Valley fold the top and bottom edges in to meet the middle fold-line.

15

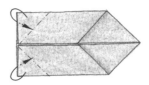

Inside reverse fold the left-hand corners.

19

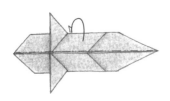

Mountain fold the paper in half from top to bottom.

20

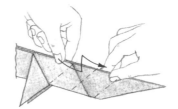

Step fold the right-hand point as shown ...

21

... to complete the tail.

16

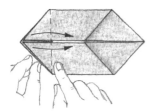

Valley fold the left-hand points (top layer only) over to the right.

17

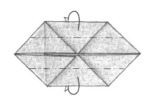

Mountain fold the top and bottom edges behind to meet the middle fold-line.

18

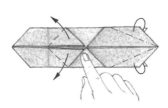

From the right-hand point, mountain fold the corners to meet the middle fold-line. Valley fold the two pointed flaps outwards.

22

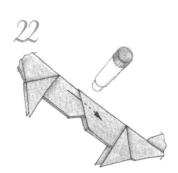

To assemble: Tuck the front section inside the back section as shown. Glue them together.

23

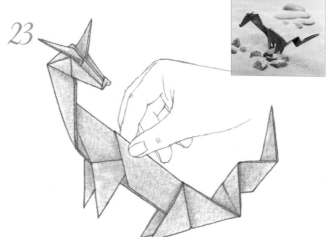

The completed green dragon.

Useful Addresses

The increasing popularity and international interest in origami is evident today in the number of organizations around the world that are devoted to it. Most paper-folding societies publish a newsletter or magazine containing origami-related articles and illustrations for new folds. They also hold regular meetings and yearly conventions that may include practical classes and exhibitions of the latest creations. They welcome folding enthusiasts of any age or level.

Origami

The following organizations offer a broad range of origami books, private publications on the various aspects of paper folding, packaged origami paper, and information on the many international origami associations.

The Membership Secretary,
British Origami Society
2a The Chestnuts, Countesthorpe,
Leicestershire LE8 5TL, England
www.britishorigami.org.uk

O.U.S.A. Center of America
15 West 77th Street, New York,
New York 10024-5192, USA
www.origami-usa.org

Visit Joseph Wu's origami website at: www.origami.vancouver.bc.ca

Japan Origami Academic Society
1-33-8-216 Hakusan,
Bunkyo-ku 113-0001, Tokyo, Japan
www.origami.gr.jp

The Nippon Origami Association
2-064 Domir Gobancho,
12 Gobancho, Chiyoda-ku,
Tokyo 102-0076, Japan
www.origami-noa.com

The Australian Origami Society
www.freewebs.com/perthorigami

Feng Shui

The Administrator,
The Feng Shui Society
377 Edgware Road,
London W2 1BT, England
www.fengshuisociety.org.uk

Further Reading

Biddle, Steve and Megumi, *Origami Inspired By Japanese Prints*, British Museum Press, in association with The Metropolitan Museum of Art, New York 1998

Kenneway, Eric, *Complete Origami*, Ebury Press, London 1987

Man-Ho Kwok, *The Feng Shui Kit*, Judy Piatkus (Publishers) Ltd, London 1995

Man-Ho Kwok, *Chinese Astrology*, Blandford, London 1997

Resources

You can purchase additional origami paper from Asian gift shops and toy stores, and also art and craft suppliers and stationers, some of which also stock textured and decorated paper. For beautifully patterned models, try using gift wrap, or to make them even more unusual, experiment with opalescent papers or paper-backed metallic foil. All kinds of paper can be used for origami – writing paper, typing paper, computer paper, and even pages cut from magazines.

Acknowledgements

We would like to thank: John Cunliffe for his assistance with writing The Origins of Origami section of this book; for sharing their original origami designs, our friends in the Nippon Origami Association: Toshio Chino, Takenao Handa, Kunihiko Kasahara, Taiko Niwa, Yasuhiro Sano, Tomoko Tanaka and the estate of Toshie Takahama; for reviewing the text, Ben Brooks, Rachael Brown and Shenna Tilley. A special thank you to Ian and Donna Carter and their family for testing the folding instructions. Credit and thanks for their creative assistance to Takeshi Morikawa and his daughter Aiko. Finally, we would like to express our gratitude to the staff at Eddison Sadd Editions.

EDDISON • SADD EDITIONS
Editorial Director....Ian Jackson
Managing Editor....Tessa Monina
Editor....Katie Ginn
Proofreader....Peter Kirkham
Art Director....Elaine Partington
Designer....Zoe Mellor
Mac Designer....Brazzle Atkins
Production....Oonagh Phelan,
                    Charles James